THE
DUMB
MEN
JOKE
BOOK

Nan Tucket

WARNER BOOKS

A Time Warner Company

WARNER BOOKS EDITION

Copyright © 1992 by Jim Mullen
All rights reserved.

Cover design by Diane Luger
Cover illustration by Bonnie Timmons

Warner Books, Inc.
1271 Avenue of the Americas
New York, NY 10020

W A Time Warner Company

Printed in the United States of America

First Printing: November, 1992

10 9 8 7 6 5 4 3 2 1

It's fun! It's easy! It's male bashing, the latest joke rage!

★

Why indulge in male bashing? Because they're just begging for it. Because you can't live with 'em and you can't live without 'em. Because they're there.

★

Is male bashing mean? *Mean? Us?* What's the matter, can't you take a joke?

★

Who can benefit from male bashing? Wives, girlfriends, daughters, sisters, mothers, nieces, working women. Hey, and men might get something out of it, too.

★

Where can you find the best male-bashing jokes?

THE DUMB MEN JOKE BOOK

Answers to the jokes on the front cover:

4. He keeps waking up every few days.

2. What page are you on?

1. Depends. How old's your husband?

3. Put the remote control between his legs.

To my male friends,
I couldn't have done this without you.
Nor would I have had to.

Acknowledgments

I'd like to thank the following men for providing the raw material for this book: Dan Quayle, Ted Kennedy, all professional wrestlers, all men named Junior and Bubba, all Congressmen, the old boy network, the Tailhook Society, and hard hats everywhere.

Introduction

Why are men so dumb? Testosterone. It appears to contain a natural IQ suppressant. Countless studies and vast bodies of anecdotal research have shown one fact to be true: the more testosterone, the dumber the man.

Many pseudo-studies contend that men are not stupid, that men and women simply communicate on different wavelengths leading each group to conclude that the other is dumb. But if you ask me, that's the beer talking. It has been proven that a man's IQ can be raised enough for basic communication skills by depriving him of beer, but that is a temporary measure and, as far as we know, no man has yet reached the intuitive communicative level of even the most average woman.

Testosterone also appears to be an hallucinogen. It makes dumb men think they are handsome and debonair when they are sitting on the La-Z-Boy eating cheeze doodles in their underwear. They think they are being Clark Gable-esque when they say things like, "Hey, babe, get us a beer, huh?" They act like they have been out hunting hairy mammoths all day when they have really spent the last eight hours in a cushy air-conditioned office with computers and fax machines. There can only be one explanation for these male fantasies. Men are in testosterone trance.

Of course, concerned women around the world have been working for years to find a cure for testosterone; but as of now, little progress has been made. We still know more about the symptoms than the disease. Some have suggested humor may be the cure, but while it seems to make women feel much better, it's effect on dumb men seems to be limited and temporary. Some dumb men are even offended by "dumb men" jokes.

What should you do if a man gets upset when you tell a "dumb man" joke? Just say, "Oh, I didn't mean 'you.'" Most men are dumb enough to believe it.

—Nan Tucket

How can you tell when a man has insomnia?
He keeps waking up every few days.

☞ ☞ ☞

How do you get a man to stop biting his nails?
Make him wear shoes.

What's the thinnest book in the world?
What Men Know About Women.

How many men does it take to screw in a light bulb?
One. Men will screw anything.

How does a man take a bubble bath?
He eats beans for dinner.

What are three little words you'll
never hear a man say?
"I'll get it."

What are three little words you'll
never hear a man say?
"It's my turn."

What are three little words you'll
never hear a man say?
"Can I help?"

☞ ☞ ☞

What's a man's idea of foreplay?
Whistling.

☞ ☞ ☞

What do you call a man with a
vasectomy?
A humanitarian.

☞ ☞ ☞

A man walks up to a parking meter
and puts in a quarter. The dial goes to
60. The man says, "Damn, I lost 100
pounds."

☞   ☞   ☞

"A woman needs a man like a fish needs a bicycle."

—Gloria Steinem

☞   ☞   ☞

Why do women rub their eyes when they wake up?

Because they don't have balls to scratch.

☞   ☞   ☞

A man saw a sign that said "Drink Canada Dry."

So he moved there.

Why is it a good thing that there are
female astronauts?
So someone will ask directions if they
get lost.

I know a man with two hundred
books and no bookcase.
I guess no one would lend him a
bookcase.

A man comes home and says to his wife, "Someone showed me an amazing device that sews buttons right on clothes."

The wife says, "That's great—what is it?"

The man says, "A needle and thread."

☞ ☞ ☞

What's the difference between an attractive woman and a proctologist?

A proctologist only has to deal with one asshole at a time.

☞ ☞ ☞

Why don't men eat more M & M's? They're too hard to peel.

☞ ☞ ☞

"My doctor says I have the breasts of an eighteen-year-old girl," a woman tells her husband.

"What did he say about your thirty-five-year-old ass?" says the man.

"I don't believe we talked about you," she replies.

☞ ☞ ☞

What do you call a man with an IQ of 50?

Gifted.

☞ ☞ ☞

What did one congressman say to the other?

What page are you on?

☞   ☞   ☞

They asked a man at the pizza parlor if he wanted his pizza cut into four pieces or eight pieces.

"Better make it four," he said, "I don't think I can eat eight."

☞   ☞   ☞

What's a man's idea of foreplay?
A half hour of begging.

☞   ☞   ☞

How can you tell if a man is sexually excited?
He's breathing.

☞ ☞ ☞

He said, "I loved you terribly."
She said, "You certainly did."

☞ ☞ ☞

What's the difference between
government bonds and men?
 Bonds mature.

☞ ☞ ☞

He said, "A lot of women are going to
be miserable when I get married."
 She said, "Really? How many women
are you planning to marry?"

☞ ☞ ☞

How long can a man live without a brain?

Depends. How old's your husband?

☞ ☞ ☞

What does a man say after his third orgasm?

"Don't you guys believe me?"

☞ ☞ ☞

"Don't tell my mother I'm in politics. She thinks I'm a prostitute."
                                    —Rep. Pat Schroeder

How do you save a man from drowning?
Take your foot off his head.

What's the most insensitive part of the penis?
The man.

How does a man turn on the light after sex?
He opens the car door.

Why are blonde jokes so short?
So men can remember them.

What do men and beer bottles have in common?
They're both empty from the neck up.

Two men are out hunting and they get into an argument.

"Those are deer tracks," one insists.

"No," says the other, "I'm sure they're elk tracks."

Just then the train hits them.

A man learned that ninety percent of all traffic accidents take place within ten miles of the home.

So he moved.

I asked my date if he had ever read Shakespeare.

He said, "No, who wrote it?"

Why did the boyfriend return his Christmas tie?
It was too tight.

Why did the man save burned-out light bulbs?
He was building a darkroom.

What does a man wear to tea?
A T-shirt.

☞ ☞ ☞

Why is it important for a woman to look her best?
Because plenty of men are stupid, but few of them are blind.

☞ ☞ ☞

Why do men have bigger brains than dogs?
So they won't hump your leg at a cocktail party.

☞ ☞ ☞

Women who want to be equal to men lack ambition.

☞ ☞ ☞

Remember, Ginger Rogers did everything Fred Astaire did—backwards in high heels.

☞ ☞ ☞

What is the ideal husband?
A guy with a $5 million life-insurance policy who dies on your wedding night.

☞ ☞ ☞

My ex is such a loser. Even Amway fired him.

❦ ❦ ❦

My husband thinks taking me to dinner at Burger King is treating me like royalty.

❦ ❦ ❦

Why do men think sex is like air? It's no big thing unless you aren't getting any.

❦ ❦ ❦

My ex will never get married again. He'll never find a woman who loves him as much as he does.

☞ ☞ ☞

Why did the woman bury her husband twelve feet under?

Because deep down he's a good person.

☞ ☞ ☞

Do you know what it means to come home to a man who'll give you a little love, a little affection, a little tenderness?

It means you're in the wrong house.

☞ ☞ ☞

A woman's place is in the House. And in the Senate.

What's a man's idea of helping with housework?
Lifting his legs so you can vacuum.

Ninety-nine percent of men give the other one percent a bad name.

What's the difference between a husband and a whale?
Whales mate for life.

If you are creative and clever, what career would your husband urge you to go into?

Keeping house.

What's the difference between a man and yogurt?

Yogurt has culture.

"Well, he's obviously a sincere man," said the first woman.

"How can you tell?"

"Who would pretend to act like an asshole?"

❦ ❦ ❦

A doctor tells a woman she has only six months to live.

"What should I do?"

"If I were you, I'd get married and move into his parents' house. It'll be the longest six months of your life."

❦ ❦ ❦

Do you know why the track at the Indy 500 is an oval?

So men won't have to stop and ask for directions.

❦ ❦ ❦

How can you tell when a man is lying?

His lips move.

☞ ☞ ☞

How can you tell if a man is happy?
Who cares?

☞ ☞ ☞

My husband says he wants to spend
his vacation someplace where he's
never been before.
I said, "How about the kitchen?"

☞ ☞ ☞

Nature abhors a vacuum. A man
abhors a vacuum cleaner.

☞ ☞ ☞

He who snores falls asleep first.

☞ ☞ ☞

How many men does it take to change
a roll of toilet paper?
We don't know. It's never happened.

☞ ☞ ☞

What happened to Roman Polanski's
last wife?
Crib death.

☞ ☞ ☞

Why does Dolly Parton resent George Bush and Dan Quayle?

Because they are the two biggest boobs in the world.

☞ ☞ ☞

Why will there be a rash of divorces in about fifteen years?

Because that's how long it will take husbands to get most of these jokes.

☞ ☞ ☞

A man goes into a drugstore and asks for a deodorant.

"The ball type?"

"No, it's for my underarms."

☞ ☞ ☞

Men don't mind dating married
women, unless it's their own.

☞ ☞ ☞

What do you call a woman who works
for a man?
The victim.

☞ ☞ ☞

What do you call a man who works
for a woman?
Damn lucky.

Why are dogs better than men?
If you get sick of a dog, you can always have it put to sleep.

How can you tell if a man is ambidextrous?
He drools from both sides of his mouth.

Why is a man like a diaper?
Because he's always on your ass and usually full of shit.

How does a man yell at his children?
"Honey, can't you keep them out of my hair?"

What's a man's idea of a seven-course meal?
A pizza and a six-pack.

A man gets in a cab and asks the driver if there's room up front for a pizza and a six-pack.
"Sure," says the driver.
So the man leans over the partition and throws up.

Why do most men think having a female vice president isn't such a bad idea?

Because we wouldn't have to pay her as much.

A man walking on the beach picks up a bottle and rubs it. Out pops a genie.

"Master, I can grant any two wishes you desire."

The man thinks for a second and says, "I want to be hard all the time and get all the ass I want."

"As you wish." There is a loud *poof* and the man turns into a toilet seat.

☞ ☞ ☞

What should a woman wear to a man's funeral?
A party dress.

☞ ☞ ☞

How does a man start a love letter?
"Did you miss me?"

☞ ☞ ☞

How do you force a man to do sit-ups?
Put the remote control between his legs.

Why do men have such big nostrils?
Just look at the size of their fingers.

What's the safest place to hide money
from a man?
Your forehead.

Why did God create man?
He couldn't teach gorillas how to
mow the lawn.

Why do men take showers instead of baths?

Peeing in a bath is disgusting.

Why do men watch football?

Because it'd be boring to talk about sex *all* the time.

A beggar walks up to a man on the street and says, "Can I have a dollar for a sandwich?"

The man says, "I don't know, let me see it."

☞ ☞ ☞

Dumb?
He thinks the English Channel is something you see on cable TV.

☞ ☞ ☞

My boyfriend and I split up because we weren't compatible.
I was a Virgo and he was an asshole.

☞ ☞ ☞

What's the difference between a man and a cat?
One is a finicky eater who couldn't care less if you lived or died; the other is a house pet.

What are the three biggest lies a woman can tell?
1) That was good. 2) I missed you. 3) It was just a wrong number.

Why do men always have stupid grins on their faces?
They're stupid.

The doctor says to the wife, "I'm giving your husband an anesthetic so he won't know anything."
"Don't bother," she says. "He doesn't know anything now."

Why did the man want to live to be 102?

He heard very few people die at that age.

THINKING
LIKE
A MAN

A Man's Diet Plan*

"Give me ten days, I'll give you ten pounds!"

Sample Menu, Day One

Breakfast
  2 Toast-em Pop-Ups
  2 Slices leftover pizza
  Coffee or tea

*Don't forget to stretch, and remember: Never start a diet without first consulting your own doctor!

Brunch
    2 breakfast burritos
    1 large fries
    2 hot apple pies
    Coffee

Lunch
    1 Big Mac
    1 large fry
    1 milk shake
    1 hot apple pie

Snack
    1 large bag Dorritos chips
    1 bag gummy bears
    1 Bud Light

Dinner Date
    3 ounces lean meat
    1 cup green vegetable
    Tossed salad
    Low-calorie dressing
    1 fruit cup
    Coffee, tea, or diet soda

Late-Night Snack
  Microwave popcorn with extra butter
  1 pint Steve's Heath Bar Crunch
  1 Bag Cheez-Its
  4 Buds

Daily Exercise
  8 hours riding around in pickup truck
  3 hours bending elbow at bar
  5.4 hours watching television

A Dictionary of Man Talk

"I'll be home in an hour."
Don't wait up.

🖝 🖝 🖝

"What do you want for your birthday?"
Hope she likes the Thighmaster.

☞   ☞   ☞

"I got stuck in traffic."
I was already late, though.

☞   ☞   ☞

"You'll never guess who I ran into."
How can I distract her from the fact
that I didn't care enough to call?

☞   ☞   ☞

"I'm on my way."
Sorry I'm late.

☞ ☞ ☞

"Did I forget our anniversary?"
I forgot our anniversary.

☞ ☞ ☞

"Home"
Where you go when the bars close.

☞ ☞ ☞

"I'm going bowling."
I'm going drinking but I can't sit still.

☞ ☞ ☞

4 × 4

My reason for living.

Anniversary Gifts
from Men

Year	Traditional	Likely Gift from a Man (if any)
1	Paper	Swatch Watch
2	Cotton	Salad Shooter
3	Leather	Crotchless Panties
4	Linen	Dustbuster
5	Wood	Jane Fonda Video
10	Tin	Weed Whacker
15	Crystal	Call Waiting
20	China	Hunting Dog
25	Silver	Carpet Shampooer
30	Pearls	Wet-Dry Vac
50	Gold	Drywall

He says to the wife, "Where is all the grocery money going?"

She says, "If you really want to know, stand sideways and look in the mirror."

The doctor told him he was overweight. He said, "No, I'm just six inches too short."

There are only two things wrong with him.

Everything he says and everything he does.

☞   ☞   ☞

He said, "People like me don't just grow on trees."

She said, "I know. They swing from them."

☞   ☞   ☞

He said, "I'm going to make you the happiest woman in the world."

She said, "I'll miss you."

☞   ☞   ☞

He said, "I want to keep you in the manner to which you're accustomed."

She said, "Thanks, but I'm tired of working."

46

☞ ☞ ☞

He said, "If anything happens to me, you'll probably have to beg for a living."
She said, "That's okay, you've given me plenty of experience."

☞ ☞ ☞

What's the definition of a bad date?
He excuses himself to call the "little woman."

☞ ☞ ☞

What's the definition of a bad date?
You pay for the dinner and he *still* runs out of gas.

Ugly?
He looks like his neck is blowing
bubble gum.

Why do men call their wives "the
little woman"?
"What? You expect me to remember
her name?"

He's economical.
He likes to save soap and water.

There's nothing he wouldn't do for me.
At least he's done nothing so far.

Why do apes hate Darwin?
They don't want people to think they're related to men.

What's he like?
How can I explain this? His dog hates him.

☞ ☞ ☞

How can you tell if a man has been in the kitchen?
The smoke.

☞ ☞ ☞

What is the one thing that doesn't fit in a modern kitchen?
An old-fashioned wife.

☞ ☞ ☞

If men had PMS . . . who could tell?

☞ ☞ ☞

What's the difference between a single mom and a married mom?
One knows exactly where the father is; the other one's just married.

   ☞ ☞ ☞

If God is a woman, who created men?

   ☞ ☞ ☞

What's a man's favorite food?
Beer.

   ☞ ☞ ☞

What's the way to a man's heart?
Who cares?

☞ ☞ ☞

What's the difference between a man and childbirth?
One is an excruciating, painful, unbearable experience; the other is just having a baby.

☞ ☞ ☞

Why do men drive pickup trucks?
So they'll have someplace to put the empties.

☞ ☞ ☞

What has eight legs and an IQ of 40?
Four guys watching football.

☞   ☞   ☞

Why did the old man have a vasectomy?
He didn't want any more grandchildren.

☞   ☞   ☞

How can you kill a man?
Put a blonde and a pickup truck in front of him and tell him he can pick one.

☞   ☞   ☞

What does a man say after sex?
Who cares?

What has hair on its chin and says "I love you"?
A parrot that just ate a mouse.

What are four little words you'll never hear a man say?
"I did the laundry."
"I washed the tub."
"I vacuumed the floor."

What has hair on its chin and says "I love you"?

Why is a beer better than a man?
Great taste, less filling.

How can you tell if a man is horny?
He's awake.

Why do men get married?
Because Mom won't put up with their shit anymore.

What's the difference between a man and a sports car?
You see a lot of cute sports cars.

☛ ☛ ☛

"A man's home may seem like his castle on the outside; inside, it's more often his nursery."

—Clare Boothe Luce

☛ ☛ ☛

"I am working for the time when unqualified blacks, browns, and women join the unqualified men in running our government."

—Cissy Farenthold

☛ ☛ ☛

"A man has to be Joe McCarthy to be called ruthless. All a woman has to do is put you on hold."

—Marlo Thomas

☞ ☞ ☞

It's hard to figure out how men think. The men in the U.S. Congress have devoted one day a year to mothers and a whole week to pickles.

☞ ☞ ☞

What was the first thing Adam said to Eve?

"Stand back! I don't know how big this thing gets."

☞ ☞ ☞

A man comes up to me with some line and says, "Can I have your phone number?"

I say, "Sure, it's in the book."

He says, "Great, and what's your name?"

I say, "That's in the book, too."

☛ ☛ ☛

Men are so filthy. I asked one guy I know if he'd done any spring cleaning. He said, "Yeah, I threw out the Christmas tree."

☛ ☛ ☛

"I will clean the house when Sears comes out with a riding vacuum cleaner."

—Roseanne Arnold

His place was so dirty I saw his dog bury a bone in his living room.

A man is outside a Las Vegas casino begging.

"Can I have $500 for my sick wife?"

A woman is walking by and says, "I'd give you the money, but how do I know you won't take it and go gambling?"

"Oh, you don't have to worry about that," he tells her, "I got gambling money."

You always hear women say that all
the best men are married or gay. Funny,
but you'd never hear a man say that
about women.

☞ ☞ ☞

Was that your boyfriend who let me
in?

Of course. Do you think I'd hire a
butler that ugly?

☞ ☞ ☞

Stupid? He wanted to be a farmer. So
he studied pharmacy.

☞ ☞ ☞

Yes, he has a hobby. He collects dust.

☞ ☞ ☞

He's so romantic. He sent me a dozen cauliflowers.

☞ ☞ ☞

He has a bumper sticker that says, "Honk if you love quiet."

☞ ☞ ☞

A man is someone who will wash his car more often than his clothes.

☞ ☞ ☞

Why do I need a husband? I already
have a dog that growls every morning, a
parrot that swears every afternoon, and
a cat that comes home late at night.

☞ ☞ ☞

His furniture is covered in plastic.
Most of it's empty food containers.

☞ ☞ ☞

"I've never been married, but I say
I'm divorced so people won't think
there's something wrong with me."
—Elayne Boosler

I had to take him to the doctor.
He had an ingrown beer can.

We went to a fancy French restaurant.
I ordered escargot.
When it came he looked at it and said,
"I'd rather eat snails."

Dumb? He asked me how to spell
I.O.U.

☞ ☞ ☞

Dumb? He asked me why I was
hanging clothes on radio antennas.

☞ ☞ ☞

He said, "I can't live without you."
She said, "Don't worry, I won't quit
my job."

☞ ☞ ☞

Why are beer cans so easy to open?
Look who's drinking them.

I called him illiterate.

He said the joke's on you, my parents were married.

What's the difference between *Newsweek* and *Playboy*?

Men look at the pictures in *Newsweek*, but they don't read the interviews.

He'll never be in "Who's Who." He may not even get into "Who?"

☞ ☞ ☞

"Macho does not prove mucho."
                                    —Zsa Zsa Gabor

☞ ☞ ☞

The only thing he can do that other people can't is read his own handwriting.

☞ ☞ ☞

No wonder men are unhappy being men. There's so little chance for advancement.

A woman is in a room at the hospital. There's a knock on the door. She says, "Come in."

A doctor comes in and says, "Please take off all your clothes."

"All of them?"

"All of them."

The doctor then gives the naked woman a thorough exam from head to toe. The doctor finishes the exam and tells the woman she can get back into bed.

"Any questions?"

"Just one," says the woman. "Why did you knock?"

She says, "How did you like those back scratchers I got you for Christmas?"

He says, "Back scratchers? I've been eating salad with them."

☞ ☞ ☞

How come men are never named Fanny?

☞ ☞ ☞

A man comes home from a hunting trip and tells his mate he shot an elk.

"Are you going to have it mounted?"

"No," he says, "I'll just keep his membership card."

☞ ☞ ☞

A man gets seriously lost on a hunting trip. Finally he runs into another hunter. "Boy am I glad to see you," he cries, "I've been lost in the cold and wet for two days!"

"Don't get too excited, good buddy," says the other hunter, "I've been lost for two weeks."

☞ ☞ ☞

He says, "I lead a dog's life."

She says, "You sure do. You come in with muddy feet, make a mess of the living room, and wait to be fed."

They're at a movie.
He says, "Can you see?"
She says, "Yes."
He says, "Is there a draft on you?"
She says, "No."
He says, "Is your seat comfortable?"
She says, "Yes."
He says, "Let's change seats."

Why do men act like such morons?
Who says they're acting?

What's the worst thing you could get on your twenty-fifth wedding anniversary?

Morning sickness.

☞ ☞ ☞

What is the soft, fleshy tissue that surrounds a penis?

A man.

☞ ☞ ☞

Did you hear about the sign someone found on the condom machine in a service station men's room? It read, "This gum tastes funny."

☞ ☞ ☞

If they can put a man on the moon,
why can't they put them all?

☞ ☞ ☞

"Talking to a man is like trying to
saddle a cow. You work like hell, but
what's the point?"

—Gladys Upham

☞ ☞ ☞

Dirty?
When he cleans his nails he loses
twenty pounds.

The rule with no exceptions: if it has tires or testicles, it'll be trouble.

"The best way to get husbands to do something is to suggest that perhaps they are too old to do it."

—Shirley MacLaine

How stupid is he?
He thinks one and one is eleven.

☞ ☞ ☞

You can tell a man that there are 300 billion stars in the universe and he will believe you. Tell him that a bench is covered in wet paint and he has to touch it.

☞ ☞ ☞

It was a man that invented the toilet seat.

It was a woman who thought of putting a hole in it.

☞ ☞ ☞

Why would someone who thinks doing laundry is complicated think I need help buying a car?

Late one night Satan shows up at a man's house and tells him he can make him the best golfer in the world.

Wary, the man says, "What do you want from me?"

Satan smacks his lips and says, "You have to let me sleep with your wife. And your teenage daughter. And your teenage son!"

The man thinks for a minute. Finally he looks at Satan and says, "What's the hitch?"

He left his body to science.
They sent it back.

☞ ☞ ☞

What do you call a man with more hair on his back than on his head?
"Honey."

☞ ☞ ☞

"Men read maps better than women because only men can understand the concept of an inch equaling a hundred miles."

—Roseanne Arnold

☞ ☞ ☞

He used to be able to lick all the kids on the block, except the Smiths. They were boys.

I called him a mophead.
He said, "Thank you."
That's when I realized he doesn't know what a mop is.

How thoughtless can a man be?
If mine won a trip for two to Paris, he'd go by himself twice.

Why don't men make ice cubes?
They can't find the recipe.

☞ ☞ ☞

Did you hear about the new parachute they've invented for smart men?

It opens on impact.

☞ ☞ ☞

Why do men like bungee jumping?

Because it takes no skill, lasts only a few seconds, and yet they can brag to their friends how good they were.

101 Uses for a Dead Man
(or a live man—sometimes it's hard to tell the difference)

Sofa Pet
Knife Holder

Silent Butler
Dumbwaiter
Shoe Rack
Donut Shop Ambience
Junk Food for Zoo Animals
Fireman on a Diesel Train
Conceptual Art
Cheap Movie Extra
City Road Repair Supervisor
Toboggan
Traffic Signal
Coatrack
Scarecrow
House Jack
Garden Hose Caddy
Birdbath
Towel Rack
Laundry Basket
Footrest
Dart Board
Anchor
Bait
Speed Bump
Absentee Dad

Booby Prize
Crash Dummy
Lamp Base
Suet
Car Chocks
Lawn Jockey
Hood Ornament
Compost Helper
Candle Snuffer
Dress Form
Sewing Table
Drywall
Novelty Rheostat
Wig Stand
Table Leaf
Curio Cabinet
Bud Vase
Luggage Rack
Fence Post
Wood Chipper Tester
Sandbag
Decorative Porch Column
Muppet
Coffee Table

Garden Nymph
Chew Toy for the Dog
Sausage Casing
Curtain Valance
Fireplace Screen
Beach Umbrella
Tea Cozy
Potpourri Pot
Front Porch Glider
Gargoyle
Drain Spout
Tractor Pull Weight
Role Model
Packing Filler
Throw Pillow
Doorman
CEO
Cake Stand
Surrogate Father
Politician
Tie Model
Candelabra
Cruelty-Free Leather
Research Cadaver

Buoy
Traffic Cone
Mobile
Elevator Counterweight
Loose-Change Container
Department Store Mannequin
Sexual Technique Instructor
Conversation Piece
Nuclear Power Plant Inspector
Father Figure
Beer Cooler Chest
Sperm Donor for People Who Don't
    Like Children
Beauty Contest Judge
Football Expert
British Lord
Postal Supervisor
Loan Officer
Miniature-Golf Obstacle
Cat Pole
Alligator Treats
Trombone Rest
Footstool
No-Skid Stair Runner

Totem Pole Replacement Parts
Surfboard Holder
Car Window Doll
Vice President

Horoscopes for Men
Good Every Day of the Year

Capricorn
This is your lucky day. Say rude and suggestive things to women as they pass on the street. Many of them will want to sleep with you no matter how disgusting you are.

Aquarius
Your day to clean. Just kidding. You don't have to do anything; you're a man.

Pisces

A good day for business even though that bad decision you made last week cost the company a fortune. Give yourself a raise and fire a couple of secretaries.

Aries

Take the day off and go drinking. Life's too short to worry about the bills. And after you're really plastered, why not drive around town and see if you can hit a loaded bus? It's okay, you're drunk. No all-male judge and jury will convict you.

Taurus

A good day to spend a lot of money at the hardware store on things you don't need. How about an electric grouter? A solder iron? A rivet gun? You can't get the car in the garage now for all the tools you've collected, so maybe it's time to buy the material you need to build a new toolshed. Shed, hell, let's build a tool Taj Mahal.

Gemini

A beautiful day to wash the car.

Cancer

Women don't understand you. That "Hey, whaddaya think, you and me, bitch" line isn't working anymore. Come to think of it, it never worked. Maybe you should stop the car the next time you yell it out the window.

Leo

Not your day for love. Don't bother bathing.

Virgo

Not a very masculine sign, is it? You lie when people ask you what your sign is, don't you? It's not nice to lie about the cosmos. You will not "get lucky" for a long time, buster.

Libra

Your day for love. Don't bother
bathing.

Scorpio

Your relationship is in trouble. Time
to spend some time patching up things
at home. Maybe you could help around
the house. Go grocery shopping. Take
the kids to a movie. Nah, why should
you both be miserable?

Sagittarius

This is your day to be spontaneous.
Maybe you should invite your friends
over for a keg party. Or maybe just go
away on a ski trip with them. Whatever
you do, don't tell the mate till things are
already in motion. Otherwise people
will think you are whipped, a fate worse
than death itself.

The Observable Universe

If you think about it, men should be the ones who ride sidesaddle.

If ties are phallic symbols, why do they sell bow ties?

Gay men and straight men have one thing in common. They both hate women.

☞ ☞ ☞

He has the body of a sixteen-year-old.
A big, fat, out-of-shape sixteen-year-old.

☞ ☞ ☞

We are working at cross-purposes
here. All men talk about are big breasts.
All the women's magazines tell women
how to get thinner thighs.

☞ ☞ ☞

Girls seldom make passes at boys
with big asses.

I'm dating a recovering workaholic. He's afraid if he ever works again, he won't be able to stop.

If we can put a man on the moon, we can get rid of SportsChannel.

Guys should remember one thing: No Christmas present should remove hair.

The Prince of Wales has the dumbest job in the world. He does for England what Goofy does for Disneyworld.

☞ ☞ ☞

He talks with his mouth full and his head empty.

☞ ☞ ☞

He wants to keep obscene art out of the galleries and on the newsstands, where it belongs.

☞ ☞ ☞

There'd be no religion if Moses had brought back the Ten Commitments.

His dining-room table was so clean you could eat off it.

He says the worst thing about sex is having to get naked in front of strangers.

How come a man's gotta do what a man's gotta do, but a cow doesn't?

☞ ☞ ☞

Why are humans the only animals
that have to teach sex to their young?

☞ ☞ ☞

I don't know how he feels about
children. All I know is that he had my
Chia Pet spayed.

☞ ☞ ☞

He says, "Running in the marathon
proves I can do something."
She says, "So does doing something."

The best thing you can say about most men is that they are biodegradable.

Only God can make a tree, but it took a man to invent dwarf-tossing.

Remember, you are known by the creep you accompany.

What do you call a sensitive,
intelligent man?
 An oxymoron.

What do you call a woman sitting
between two men?
 An interpreter.

How do men define a long-term
relationship?
 A second date.

🖝 🖝 🖝

What do you call a man who complains all day, watches sports all night and sleeps away his weekends?
Normal.

🖝 🖝 🖝

How many men does it take to change a mind?
None. Once their minds are made up they never change.

🖝 🖝 🖝

How do you know when a man is trying to make a fashion statement?

The brim of his baseball cap is turned backwards.

🖝 🖝 🖝

What's the difference between a sixteen- and a thirty-five-year-old man?

A mortgage, two credit cards and a forehead.

🖝 🖝 🖝

What's the difference between a wise man and a dumb man?

Absolutely nothing. They both think they know everything.

☞   ☞   ☞

What do you call a man who gets his own beers between innings?

Athletic.

☞   ☞   ☞

What do you call a man who drives with one hand on the wheel, one hand on the radio, a beer between his knees, and both eyes leering at a girl walking along the sidewalk?

Safety conscious. At least he has one hand on the wheel.

☞   ☞   ☞

What's the difference between men and chimpanzees?

One is hairy, smelly, and picks his butt; the other can be taught to communicate with human beings.

What's the difference between men and pigs?

One likes to eat, sleep, burp, and roll in the mud; the other is considered intelligent, and has a curly tail and a snout.

Dan Quayle Jokes

Dan Quayle heard we only use a quarter of our brain.

"What," he asked, "do we do with the other quarter?"

❧ ❧ ❧

They asked Dan Quayle to spell Mississippi.

He said, "You can't trick me again. The river or the state?"

❧ ❧ ❧

How dumb is Dan Quayle?

Barbara Bush won't give him a puppy until he proves he can take care of it himself.

☞ ☞ ☞

Dan Quayle wants to visit Nicaragua to see the falls.

☞ ☞ ☞

Dan Quayle is so dumb, he thinks that paramedics and paralegals come from Paraguay.

☞ ☞ ☞

How does Dan Quayle spell "farm"? E-I-E-I-O . . . E

About the Author

Nan Tucket likes to bicycle, play tennis, and give remedial reading lessons to Playboy models and the men who love them.